For Jeff and Judy
DR

For Ian—my love, my friend—
who can play all the hits on a
single blade of grass
SC

Special thanks to Carter Hasegawa, Hilary Van Dusen, and Marietta Zacker

. . .

Text copyright © 2024 by Dean Robbins
Illustrations copyright © 2024 by Susanna Chapman

First edition 2024

Library of Congress Catalog Card Number pending
ISBN 978-1-5362-2486-3

APS 28 27 26 25 24 23
10 9 8 7 6 5 4 3 2 1

Printed in Humen, Dongguan, China

This book was typeset in Georgia.
The illustrations were created with watercolor, gouache, cut paper, and a digital zhuzh.

Candlewick Press
99 Dover Street
Somerville, Massachusetts 02144

www.candlewick.com

The FASTEST DRUMMER

CLAP YOUR HANDS FOR VIOLA SMITH!

DEAN ROBBINS

illustrated by
SUSANNA CHAPMAN

CANDLEWICK PRESS

Five girls played together
in the Smith Sisters Orchestra.
Irene on trombone.
Erma on vibraphone.
Edwina on trumpet.
Mildred on violin.
Lila on saxophone.

Was there a spot for the sixth sister, Viola?
Almost every instrument was taken . . .

except the drums.

Viola tried out a **RAT-TAT-TAT** on the snare.

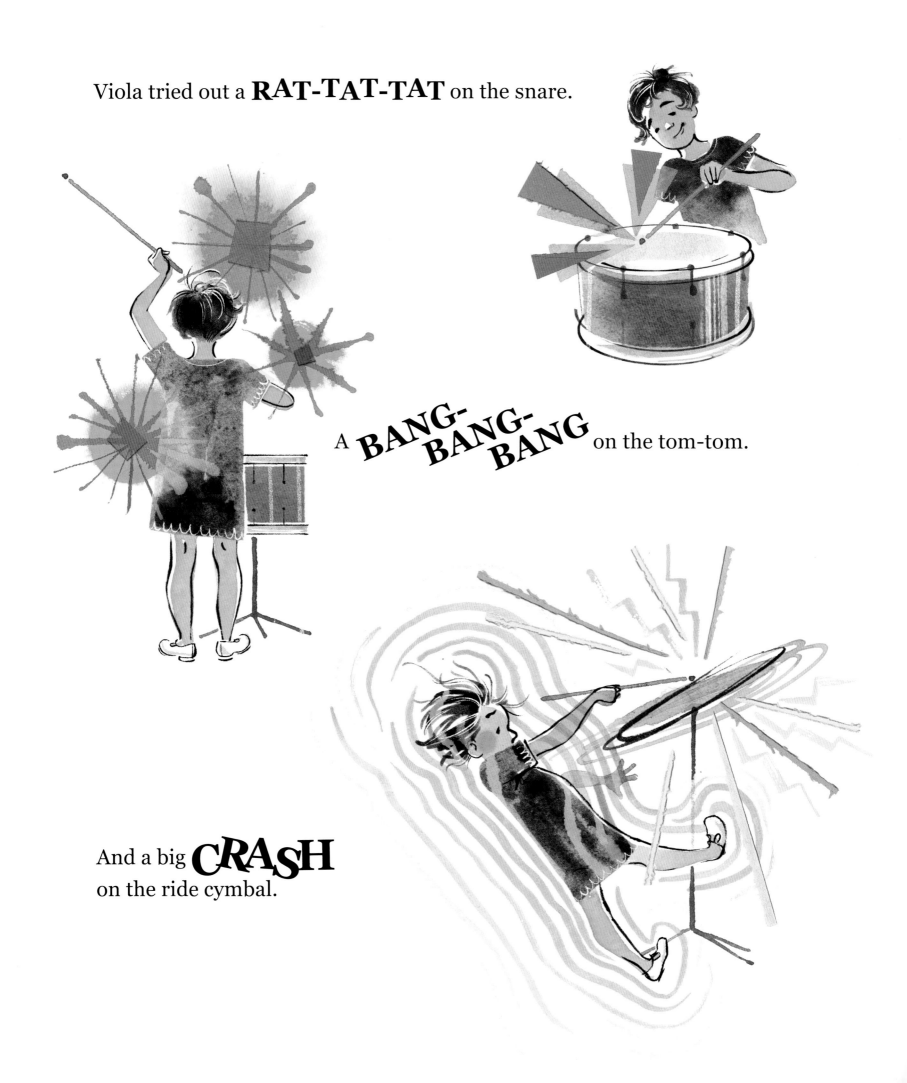

A **BANG-BANG-BANG** on the tom-tom.

And a big **CRASH** on the ride cymbal.

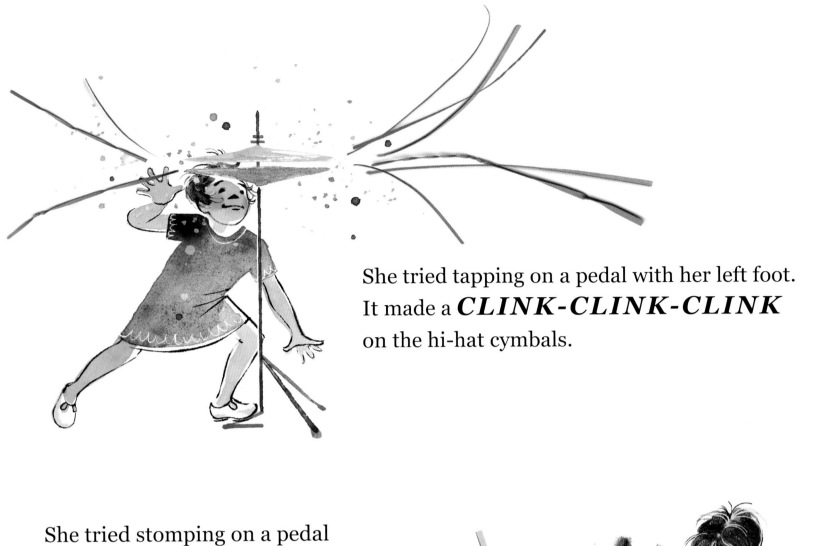

She tried tapping on a pedal with her left foot.
It made a **CLINK-CLINK-CLINK**
on the hi-hat cymbals.

She tried stomping on a pedal
with her right foot.
It made a **BOOM**
on the bass drum.

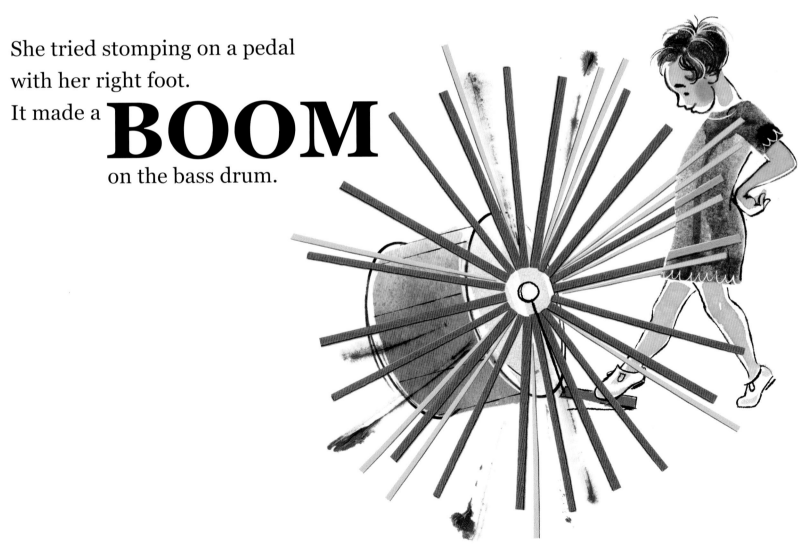

The sisters started a song, and Viola tried keeping up with them.

She lost the beat,
made a terrible racket,
and had more fun than she'd ever had before!

Papa showed her the proper
way to hold the sticks.

The Smith Sisters Orchestra entertained friends and family in Mount Calvary, Wisconsin. They played a lively style called **jazz** in Papa's small-town ballroom.

Each girl took a solo, making up music on the spot.

Viola always looked forward to her turn. She liked being **bold** and **flashy** and *fast!*

Dancers whirled and twirled to her galloping rhythms.

Two younger sisters joined the group, Loretta on piano and Sally on saxophone. In the 1920s, all eight girls began to travel around the Midwest, playing for bigger and bigger crowds.

Thirteen-year-old Viola loved watching other bands on stage, especially the drummers.

After each show, she introduced herself and asked for musical advice.

"How do you make your hands and feet work well together?"

"How do you play loud without drowning out the other instruments?"

"How do you play fast without losing the beat?"

They were happy to answer her questions.

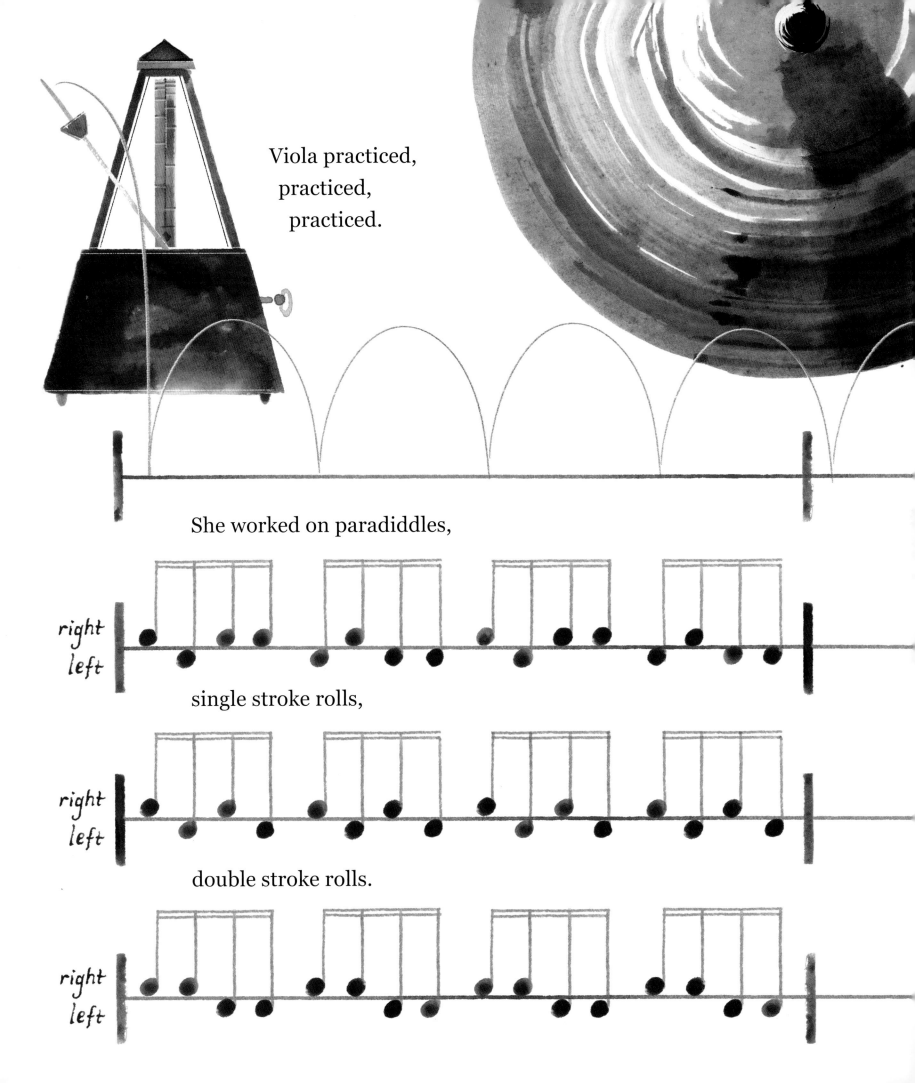

Viola practiced,
practiced,
practiced.

She worked on paradiddles,

right
left

single stroke rolls,

right
left

double stroke rolls.

right
left

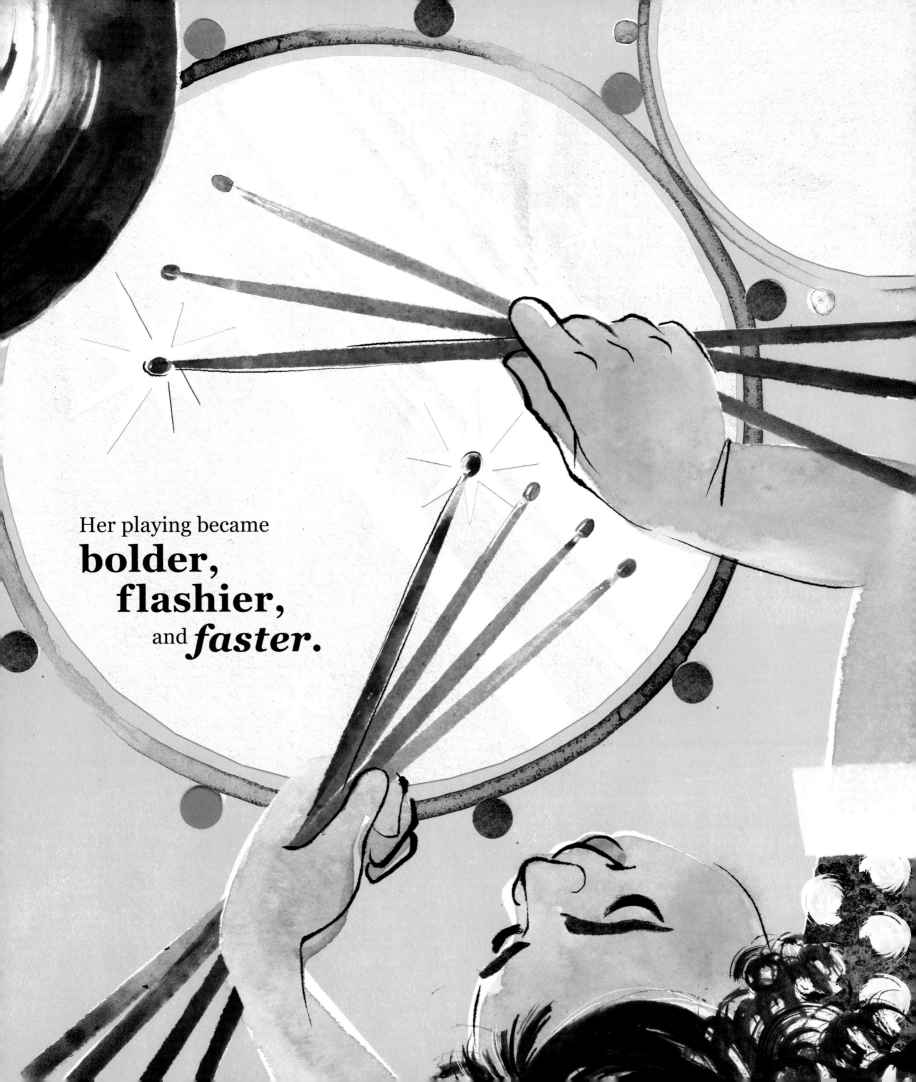

Her playing became **bolder, flashier,** and *faster.*

The Smith sisters grew up
and lost interest in the band.
One by one, they left to do other things.
But Viola did not want to do something else.
She lived for making music.
How could she find work as a drummer?

Women musicians got little respect in the 1930s.
Male bands would not hire them.
Music companies would not record them.
Most listeners did not take them seriously.
They believed women could never sound as good
as men did on their instruments.

Viola had an idea for changing people's minds. She would start her own women's band: The Coquettes! Her sister Mildred agreed to come along for the new adventure.

First, Viola put together a spectacular drum kit with twelve pieces. Then she placed it on a high platform, with a big drum hanging near each shoulder. No one had ever done that before.

She smacked the snare and smashed the cymbals.
Her left foot hammered the hi-hat pedal.
Her right foot bashed the bass-drum pedal.
She rapped out rhythms on the two big drums by her shoulders.

To end a song, she bounced her drumsticks off the tom-tom and leaped up to catch them in midair.

"Clap your hands FOR VIOLA

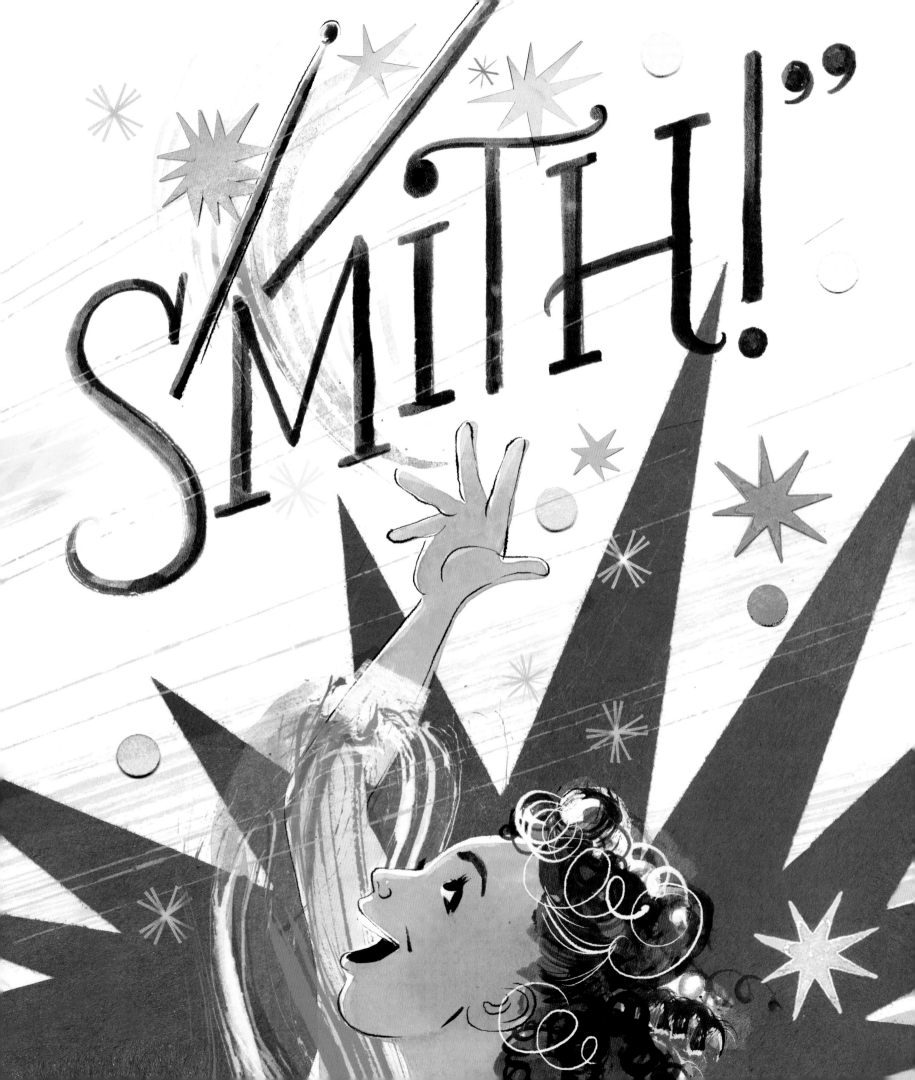

The Coquettes soon became famous.
They performed in movies and on radio.
Viola even appeared on a magazine cover.

At every show, she proved she could play as well as any man.
And faster than just about everybody.
People hailed her as "the fastest girl drummer in the world"!

What about the other talented women hoping to succeed in
the music business? Viola yearned to help them out.

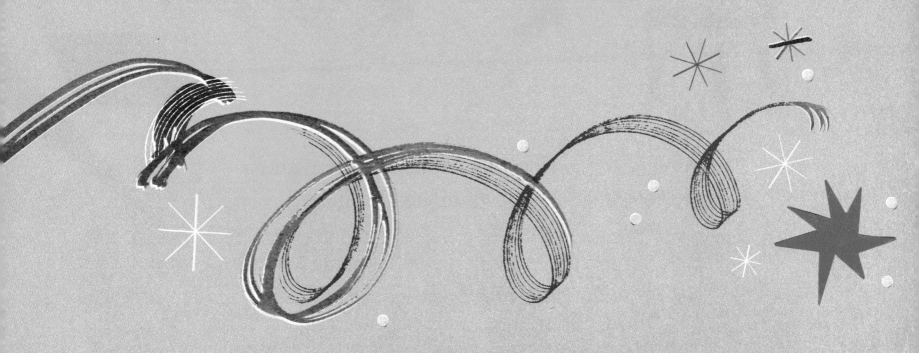

When a war started in 1941, she saw her chance.
Men began leaving bands to join the military,
and Viola knew exactly who could take their places.
"Why not let the girls play in the big-name bands?"
she wrote in a magazine article.

Give Girl Musicians a Break!

They are as much the masters of their instruments as are male musicians. Their solos show unlimited imagination. Now is the time for all girl musicians to seek to be recognized!

Thousands of people read Viola's article.
Music companies talked about it.
Bandleaders thought about it.
And women acted on it.
More and more of them joined groups,
made records, and gained loyal fans.

Viola led the way by playing with the world's best musicians.

She made friends with the world's best drummers, too. They gave each other musical advice.

She started a solo act and added five pieces to her spectacular drum kit.

VIOLA & HER 17 DRUMS

Viola continued to practice, practice, practice. She went to college to master a type of drum called timpani. Symphony orchestras invited her to play classical music.

In 2000, America celebrated Viola
as a musical legend.

But she wasn't done yet.

At the age of 100, she was still slamming
her snare and socking her cymbals.

AUTHOR'S NOTE

When Viola Smith (1912–2020) was growing up, everybody listened to jazz. But most people thought only male instrumentalists should play this popular style of music. They considered it unladylike for women to blow trumpets, trombones, and saxophones—or, like Viola, to beat on drum kits. They also assumed that women could not master such difficult instruments.

Because men did not usually play with female instrumentalists, Viola and others began to form their own jazz bands in the 1920s and '30s. Along with the Coquettes, all-women groups included the International Sweethearts of Rhythm, the Darlings of Rhythm, Ina Ray Hutton's Melodears, and the Prairie View Co-Eds.

The women proved their skills, but they still struggled to gain respect in the music business. That changed in the 1940s, when many men left their bands to fight in World War II. Viola spoke out boldly in a 1942 article called "Give Girl Musicians a Break!," arguing that women were well qualified to take their places. The article made a big impression on readers, and doors started opening for women. Trombonist Melba Liston joined the Gerald Wilson band, trumpeter Billie Rogers joined Woody Herman's Herd, and saxophonist Elsie Smith joined the Lionel Hampton Orchestra, among others.

Viola herself received many offers to play in other bands. She performed with jazz greats like Chick Webb and Ella Fitzgerald and starred with the famous Hour of Charm Orchestra. She appeared in movies, in theaters, on television, on radio, and at the inauguration of President Harry Truman, and was billed as "the fastest girl drummer in the world." She befriended top male drummers like Gene Krupa, Buddy Rich, and Jo Jones, who loved to hear her perform.

Viola never stopped developing her skills. She took lessons in jazz drumming and studied classical music at the Juilliard School of Music. She also worked as a percussionist in the National Symphony Orchestra and the NBC Symphony Orchestra. Throughout her life, she enjoyed playing different kinds of music with diverse musicians, regardless of whether they were Black or white, male or female.

Following Viola's lead, countless women instrumentalists made their mark on popular music. They hailed her as a hero and an inspiration, marveling at her determination to keep playing to the age of 107.

I live near Mount Calvary, Wisconsin, where young Viola learned to play the drums. And long before I was born, she performed in my hometown with the fabulous Smith Sisters Orchestra (originally called the Schmitz Sisters Orchestra). As a lifelong jazz fan and trumpet player, I'm proud of my small connection to this musical legend!

MUSICAL TERMS

Beat: A musical rhythm.

Double stroke roll: A drumbeat that quickly alternates two strokes from one drumstick, then two strokes from the other, in the order of left-left-right-right.

Jazz: An artful style of popular music featuring bold rhythms. Jazz songs are built around improvisation, which means making up music on the spot rather than playing written notes.

Paradiddle: A drumbeat of four even strokes of the drumstick, in the order of right-left-right-right or left-right-left-left.

Percussion: Instruments, such as drums, that make a sound when struck, shaken, plucked, or rubbed.

Rhythm: The pattern of sounds that makes music flow.

Single stroke roll: A drumbeat that quickly alternates one stroke from each drumstick, in the order of left-right-left-right.

Solo: A section of music that features a single player. In jazz, musicians often make up their solos through improvisation.

RESOURCES

Chaikin, Judy, director. *The Girls in the Band*. Virgil Films, 2015, DVD.

Dahl, Linda. *Stormy Weather: The Music and Lives of a Century of Jazz Women*. New York: Limelight Editions, 1989.

The International Sweethearts of Rhythm. *Hot Licks: 1944–46*. Sounds of Yesteryear, 2005, CD.

Placksin, Sally. *American Women in Jazz: 1900 to the Present*. New York: Seaview Books, 1982.

Shadwick, Keith. *The Illustrated Story of Jazz*. New York: Chartwell Books, 1995.

Smith, Angela. *Women Drummers: A History from Rock and Jazz to Blues and Country*. Lanham, Maryland: Rowman & Littlefield, 2014.

Smith, Viola. "Give Girl Musicians a Break!" *Down Beat*, February 1, 1942.

Tucker, Sherrie. *Swing Shift: "All-Girl" Bands of the 1940s*. Durham, North Carolina: Duke University Press, 2000.

Vadukul, Alex. "Viola Smith, 'Fastest Girl Drummer in the World,' Dies at 107." *New York Times*, November 6, 2020.

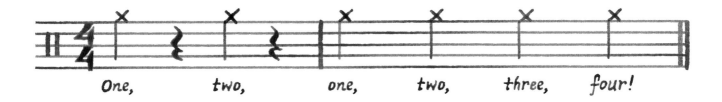